THE DEBT FREE PHYSICIAN

A Doctor's Guide to getting out of debt fast and surviving your first year

Kamala Gordon, MD, MBA

ILLUMINATION PRESS
Atlanta,Georgia

THE DEBT FREE PHYSICIAN

A Doctor's Guide to Getting Out of Debt and Surviving Your First Year

Paperback ISBN: 978-1-950681-14-3
Ebook ISBN: 978-1-950681-03-7

Cover and Interior Design by AugustPride, LLC

ILLUMINATION PRESS
1100 Peachtree Street, Suite 250
Atlanta, Georgia 30309
United States

www.illuminationpress.com

TABLE OF CONTENTS

INTENTION

Your first year as an attending or independent physician will be the most challenging. You have worked and practiced under direct guidance and supervision during Residency and Fellowship training. Now, you are free to make decisions independently. With your career in your hands and all your years of studies leading up to this moment, every decision is important—your family, career, and patients depend on you.

This is the year the student loan companies will expect you to start paying back your loans. Your grace period is over.

This is the year you will learn that being a physician is not only about treating patients, but it's also about meeting the standards hospitals set for you which are the same standards that the insurance companies require for your hospital to be reimbursed.

This is the year, if you don't work and negotiate smart, you will likely be burned out.

This is the year you will answer your own question—Why did I choose medicine?

Most importantly -

This is the year you could pay off your debts and begin living a life of financial freedom and ultimate success.

While medical school might prepare you for the grueling days of long hours and intensive work you will do as a physician, your medical school training is woefully inadequate when it comes to preparing you for financial success.

Doctors, even with their prestigious positions and exorbitant salaries, are not immune to the crushing weight of student loan debt. The average doctor graduates medical school with more than $200,000 in debt. Yet, medical school doesn't teach you about how to get out of debt. They don't teach you that making the minimum payments on your loans will have you in debt for the rest of your life chained to a career that becomes a burden instead of a dream. I decided early on that I didn't want that nightmare to be my reality.

One year after I graduated from residency, I became a Debt Free Physician. Being debt free allows me the opportunity to do the work I love, not because I have to, but because I want to. This book is about my journey and how you can do it too. I invite you to join me in living a debt free life.

What I want you to take away by reading this book is that to become debt free you can't live the way people expect you to live because you are a "Doctor" now, at least not for a little while. If you live like an undergraduate student during your medical and training years, you will be able to live like a "Doctor" without being financially strapped to your employer.

What I realize is that when you become a licensed physician and have debt, sometimes you may choose to stay in a position you don't like because of your obligation to your debt. You may also sacrifice time with your family due to a debt obligation. Some physicians even put off having children because of their debt burden. Being in debt can make you sign contracts with five years or more of commitment to a position you hate because your employer offers you loan forgiveness.

This book is written to highlight the various options available so you can practice medicine how and when you want to, instead of practicing it to cover your debt. I always wanted to practice medicine how I chose to and not because I have debt to pay off. If this is your goal, then consider reading this book. You don't want to buy a house you can't live in because you are busy working or have a family that you can't see because of debt. You sacrificed more than 30 years in studies and training, why not get out of debt and enjoy the rest of your life on your own time how you see fit.

THE DEBT FREE PHYSICIAN

I had finally finished my fellowship in Geriatrics, and now it was time to look for my dream career. During my job search, I realized there were many different models for Geriatrics— academic opportunities to teach in a hospital setting; house visits; nursing home rounds; and weekend on-call service. These options offered different duties and responsibilities, but they were all lumped under one salary. I was also researching hospitalist opportunities since I am Board Certified in Internal Medicine as well as a second option. I realized that a lot of companies required working experience for hospital work. I didn't want to lose my in-patient skills so I decided to look for a career in hospital medicine just so I could have some work experience on my resume before I chose to start my career off as a Geriatrician, which would entail mostly nursing homes, office and consulting. I also listened to my friends who were complaining to me that they were forgetting some of their hospital skills while working inside an office setting. Some of my friends who worked in the Southern United States where family medicine doctors working as hospitalists and told me that they could work more hours and felt freer working as a hospitalist than in an office setting. With this in mind, I decided to start my career off as a Nocturnist.

Being a night-time physician paid a higher salary than day work, and there was less micromanagement and administration at night. The first contract I signed was with a hospitalist staffing company. I still had several months before I would officially begin working, but I wanted to lock down my job options as soon as I possibly could. In a rush to have a secured position, I signed the contract within just a few days of my interview without having a lawyer review it. A few months before I was to begin my work, I got a call stating, "Sorry Doc, our Hospitalist Staffing Company lost the contract with the hospital you were scheduled to work. We would like you to work at another hospital 40 minutes away."

I did not want to make such a long commute, so I rejected the staffing company's offer. Since I had not yet started working for the staffing company, I sought to work directly for the hospital previously under contract with the staffing company. This was when I learned my first lesson in non-solicitation agreements and restrictive covenants. When the hospitalist staffing company learned that I was inquiring about working for the hospital, I signed up with, and they informed me that I would not be able to work with that hospital unless the hospital paid them because they found me first. Eventually, I was able to get my contract annulled since I never actually started working for them, and I was able to secure a new job with a different company.

When I received my first paycheck, I was excited, but I didn't want to spend it. I wanted to put it all on my student loans. I had been living from paycheck to paycheck. It was something I'd watched my parents do my entire life, and I was sick of it. So, instead of blowing my entire paycheck on a new wardrobe, I decided to continue wearing my scrubs to work—after all, I wasn't getting a stipend to look cute.

If you will live like no one else, later you can live like no one else.

• Dave Ramsey •

For twelve months, I worked as a W-2 fulltime employee, picking up extra shifts in between my seven nights on, seven nights off schedule. Even though I was a W-2 employee, I got paid per shift—the more shifts I worked, the more money I made.

Living frugally and working as much as I could paid off.

I started working at the end of August 2017 and was debt free by the second week of September 2018. It was a huge accomplishment. In just one year, I had become 100% totally debt free! No more student loans. No more bill collectors. Now, all of the money I made could be saved and invested in making me even more money. Now, I could loosen up my purse strings and buy some of the things I wanted without feeling guilty or digging myself deeper into debt. This freedom opened up so many doors for me—and I want the same for you too.

A WORD OF CAUTION

My year-long journey to debt freedom took a lot out of me, not just physically, but emotionally and mentally as well. I was drained and burned out.

Making the commitment to get out of debt is a decision you should not take lightly. Before you begin your journey, you must acknowledge the sacrifices you are willing to make.

This will not be easy.

There will be times when you feel as if the sacrifice you are making is too much.

When you see your friends and colleagues living lavishly, while you're driving the same car you've been driving since college, you might be tempted to cave in and give up before you've reached the goal line.

Don't do it! Be willing to make the sacrifice now so that later on, you will be able to truly enjoy a rich and fulfilling life.

That's exactly what I want for you—a rich, prosperous, and fulfilling life doing the work you love.

And guess what?

Because I've made it to the elusive land of debt freedom, I can guide you through the proves, helping you to navigate all the landmines on the way.

After having endured the arduous and back-breaking task of paying off my student loan debts in one year, I learned several valuable lessons. I can admit that even with my success in attaining debt freedom, there were things I could have done that would have possibly allowed me to not only pay off my debt sooner but also made the time a lot less stressful and overwhelming.

Now, I am passing these lessons on to you. The tips and strategies in this book will help you become a Debt Free Physician faster than you ever imagined.

THE DEBT TRAP

The Big Myth

There is a huge myth about physicians that I want to address right from the start. Most people assume that physicians are rich. The high salaries, seemingly luxurious living, and the portrayal of physicians on television and in the media perpetuate this myth.

The truth is far less glamorous.

While physicians are among the most revered and highest paid professionals, there is a sad truth that most won't admit. The truth is—most physicians are faring no better, and in some cases are doing worse, than the average American—drowning in debt and living paycheck to paycheck.

However, instead of shedding light on the reality of their condition, most physicians feed into the wealthy doctor stereotype and fall further and further into the debt trap to keep up the lie.

Snared by the Debt Trap

It's not all your fault, though.

Banks, car dealerships, credit card companies—they all are eager to keep you focused on keeping up with the Dr. Joneses. As soon as you complete your medical training and are in your first year after residency and fellowship, the zeroes in your paycheck begin to multiply exponentially. Now instead of making a choice between top ramen and spaghetti-o's you can eat at a five-star restaurant and order the filet mignon and lobster. Knowing that you have much more disposable income, car dealerships and realty companies send targeted ads your way making your Toyota Corolla, and studio apartment feel cramped and uncomfortable. Banks and mortgage companies tempt you with huge lines of credit and mortgage loans that require no mortgage insurance and zero-down-payment on a house.

On top of all the financial pressure, your family and friends chime in with the expectations of your next steps. Now that you have your career settled, it's only natural that you start to think of marriage and a family, right? After all, you are in your thirties now, and you are not getting any younger.

With all of the financial and societal pressure of living up to everyone else's expectations, it is no wonder that most physicians fall into the debt trap. But that doesn't have to be you.

In the next section, I will share with you the secrets to breaking free of the debt trap so that you can truly have the life you desire. Before I do that, however, I want to give you the Golden Rule of being a Debt Free Physician. If you follow this rule and the strategies I share in the next section, you will eliminate your debt and have the financial freedom you desire faster than you ever imagined.

"If you live like a poor physician for a few years in the beginning, you'll be a wealthy debt free physician for the rest of your life."

• Kamala Gordon, MD, MBA•

Don't make big purchases right away.

It's your first real job outside of training. Get into the rhythm of making more money and become adjusted to your new standard of living before you buy your dream car or purchase a million-dollar mansion. If you spend too much too soon, you'll find yourself drowning in payments you can't handle and may end up losing what you have worked so hard for.

Be intentional about paying down your student loan debt.

It won't go away if you don't look at it. It will increase by compound interest. The interest will add to the principal, and your debt balance will just continue to increase.

Live on less than you make.

Try to live like a resident for at least one more year after training until you figure out the direction you want to go in and if your new job is the best fit for you. Instead of spending your entire paycheck, save as much as you can, and build an emergency fund that can cover your expenses for at least six months. Pay down your debt to create a financial cushion for yourself before making large purchases.

THE PATH TO DEBT FREEDOM

After escaping the debt trap, I made it my mission to help others do the same. Like Harriet Tubman, I want to use this book as a vehicle to lead as many physicians as I can to debt freedom.

As you read this section, take note of the tips and strategies I share with you. I've traveled the road and mapped the course so you can avoid the pitfalls and roadblocks that keep so many in bondage to debt.

RESIDENCY

The decisions you make during Residency will determine the course of your financial future. The money habits you develop now will not only help you to achieve freedom from your student loan debt faster than you ever imagined; it will also allow you to maintain your financial freedom for the rest of your life.

Do you remember the Golden Rule? Well, I first started using it during my Residency. Even though I was starting to make some money, I lived as frugally as possible. I wore scrubs to save money on clothing. I lived walking distance to the hospital where I worked so I didn't need a car. I had roommates to save money on rent.

I'll admit—it wasn't easy living this way, especially when my colleagues were starting to buy fancy new cars and wearing designer labels. But I wouldn't trade places with them. I am totally debt free and able to purchase anything I want now.

How to Best Use Your Resident Salary

The salary you will earn as a resident depends on the location you choose. The highest paid residency is usually located in highly populated inner-city areas and community hospitals that need to attract good candidates. Most residents will tell you that they choose their area of specialty based on potential earnings. However, I would advise against that. You will be sacrificing a lot of your life and time, working long, hard hours as a resident. Doing work, you don't really enjoy just to have a few hundred more dollars in your paycheck isn't worth it. In the end, your mental and emotional health are much more valuable than that.

The best thing to do is to choose the specialty you most want to work in and then use the strategies I share to make that salary work for you and your goal of getting out of debt.

- If you choose a lower paying residency program and cannot afford the principal and interest payments, try paying off your interest only. This will keep your student loan balance from going up.
- If you choose a higher paying residency program, try to cover your principal and interest if possible. This will lower your student loan balance at the end.
- Consider joining the National Health Service Corps to start obtaining money towards your debt and place the full amount on your student loans. (You'll learn more about this program in the next section.)
- Consider refinancing your student loans for a lower interest rate. Some refinance companies do not give more than a two-week grace period if you default on paying back the said amount due to hardships.
- Wear scrubs. Don't try to spend lots of money on new clothes.
- Live close to the hospital where you are doing a residency to cut down the cost of a commute.

- Consider roommates to cut down the costs of your living expenses. If roommates aren't a feasible option for you, get a studio instead of a three-bedroom apartment.
- Obtain practice procedure-based skills during training. Jobs that require procedures pay more than non-procedural jobs. For example, Central Lines, Intubation, Paracentesis, Lumbar Punctures.
- When possible, buy your groceries and other essential items in bulk to save money.

NHSC AND YOUR LOANS

State funded projects such as the National Health Service Corps (NHSC) loan repayment program offer opportunities to pay off your student loans in exchange for working a minimum of two years in underserved areas. You can sign up for the NHSC loan repayment program during medical school through their student to the service program. These contracts are great but sometimes they will start you off at a low base salary and would offer yearly installments on your student loans as long as you agree to stay and work for additional years. There is also a requirement to work full-time for three years but you can work outside of this agreement as long as you have completed your obligations.

This opportunity is great if you are the type that has a hard time keeping up with bills and like the idea that someone else is paying it for you while you only have to budget your base salary and not have to think about your student loans. They will also start paying off your student debt while you are in Residency training if you sign up early and continue installments during your two to three-year obligation.

Here is a trick to quickly pay down your debt even faster: each installment given to you should be deposited entirely on your loan. For example— $30,000 checks may be handed to you each year once you sign up for the program. You should deposit all of this on your student loan at once to decrease your principal balance immediately and use your residency income or attending salary to make monthly installments on your student loan interest and debt. If you receive a check of $30,000 per year for 6 years (3 years during residency and 3 years of working in an underserved area) this will equal to $180,000 down over 6 years but the trick is to put each yearly installment all at once while you continue to make routine monthly payments.

A friend of mine divided his $30,000 check into monthly payments and regrets doing that because this only prolonged his loan repayment causing the banks to make more money off him through interest.

CHOOSING THE RIGHT DEBT REPAYMENT METHOD

The Avalanche Method

If you have multiple loans with different interest rates, the Avalanche Method is for you. This strategy is useful if you focus on getting rid of high-interest debt first. List your debts in order from highest interest rate to the lowest interest rate. Starting at the top devote as much cash as possible to the highest interest rate loan first, while making minimum payments on the other debts. Once you wipe it out, move to the loan with the second highest interest rate.

Pay off private loans first due to the usually highest interest rates and less flexible repayment terms than federal loans. If you have both, you'll likely want to focus on these first. If you sign up for variable interest rates, these may rise over time, so I would recommend paying these off first.

The Snowball Method

Another method is to prioritize your debt according to the balance owed, regardless of interest rate. List your debts in order from smallest to the largest and start paying off the one with the lowest balance. The Snowball Method will motivate you to keep paying off your debt continuously. Once you've paid off the smallest loan while making minimum payments on the rest, move on to the second lowest balance. It may not save you as much on interest, but it is sure to keep you motivated.

Refinancing

Consider refinancing multiple loans through consolidation and lowering your interest rate, so more of your payment goes to the principal. I refinanced my private student loans during residency and my interest rate went from 9.9% down to 6.115%. You will also save 0.25% if you sign up for automatic direct withdrawal during your payments. One of my colleagues had an interest rate as low as 2% from a Canadian bank. Do your research and look for the lowest interest rate possible.

New York and Free Medical School

If you are reading this book after you've already completed medical school, this section won't be applicable to you. However, you should read it and pass the information on to younger friends and family members who are considering medical school. It will be very valuable for them.

In April 2018, NYU School of Medicine announced that it would cover the tuition of all its students, regardless of merit or need, due to the "overwhelming financial debt" facing graduates. In the past, much effort was focused on helping undergraduates cover the balance of their tuition bills, including community colleges in Tennessee, and two and four-year schools in New York (CUNY and SUNY) under the New Excelsior Scholarship.

Schools have become worried that students saddled with steep debt are increasingly pursuing top-paying specialties rather than careers in family medicine, pediatrics, and research. Columbia also announced a $250 million gift from an alumnus to benefit medical students with the highest financial need, full-tuition scholarships, and other student grants, rather than loans.

BEWARE OF PUBLIC SERVICE LOAN FORGIVENESS

If you have federal student loans, the Public Service Loan Forgiveness program might be something you have considered for eliminating your student loan debt. In exchange for working in the public sector or practicing with a non-profit organization, this program will pay off the balance of your student loans after 10 years. It sounds like a great idea—right?

Maybe.

There are many factors you must consider before you enter into an agreement for the Public Student Loan Forgiveness program. Failure to fully understand the requirements and regulations could be a costly mistake.

While there is great benefit to the Public Service Loan Forgiveness program, there are drawbacks too. Before you make a commitment to this type of loan repayment program do your research and understand exactly what you are signing up for.

To qualify for PSLF, you must make 120 qualifying payments (10 years) on Direct Loans while employed full-time by a qualifying employer. Qualifying employers include governmental agencies or tax-exempt organization under Section 501(c)(3) of the Internal Revenue Code. If your employer is a partisan political organization or a labor union, your employer will not qualify. If the organization that you work for full-time switches to a for-profit organization at any time during the ten years under your agreement, your loan payments will be disqualified for forgiveness.

One of my colleagues experienced this personally—after making four years of qualifying payments his hospital decided to go from a non-profit to a for-profit institution and now, instead of having only six years left to qualify for full loan forgiveness, he has to start all over from the beginning.

Unfortunately, my colleague's predicament is quite normal. Regulations for qualification under the Public Service Loan Forgiveness program are very rigorous. Only one percent of borrowers who apply for loan forgiveness under the program are approved. After working ten years of public service, twenty-eight thousand professionals applied for loan forgiveness in 2018. Only ninety-six of them were approved. That means less than one percent of all professions who complete the PSLF program actually receive loan forgiveness.

In order to avoid this dilemma, the PSLF program recommends you complete an Employment Certification each year to make sure you are still making progress to qualify for loan forgiveness.

A Word About Income Based Repayment

To help you stay current with your student loan payments, loan companies will offer you the option of choosing a payment plan based on your income. Choosing this option will lower your monthly payments. This option is good in the short term but devastating to your financial future in the long run. Here's why—the lower payment amount barely covers the interest on the loan and does not reduce the principal balance at all. Therefore, although you are making timely payments each month, the interest you are not able to cover with the lower payments is being added to the principal balance, thus increasing the amount you owe. It's a vicious cycle and can add decades to your loan repayment.

If you combine the income-based repayment plan with a Public Service Loan Forgiveness program, you must be even more careful. If your loan forgiveness does not meet qualification standards during the ten years, it is as if you haven't paid anything and you will need to start from scratch. With the additional interest added to your principal, your loan amount will be higher. Imagine paying your loans for four years and four years after you started your loan amount is even higher than what you started with.

STUDENT LOANS AND PURCHASING YOUR FIRST HOME

I would recommend living in your parents' basement or your old bedroom (as long as you can get along with your family) for at least a year or two until you can start eliminating debt and saving up for a sizeable down payment on your first home.

Your student loans are considered a liability to the banks, and if you want a low-interest rate, it may not be possible with high debt. You have lived like a resident for a few years already, one or two more years living like a resident may still be doable and less stressful financially in the long run.

Before purchasing a home make sure you run your credit report not just your credit score. If your family took out a credit card in your name and it went to a collection agency or you have delayed or delinquent payments, this may affect your mortgage interest rates. If you have payments to be made on your vehicle, this will also be considered a liability and affect your debt to income ratio. Your debt to income ratio is all your liabilities such as mortgages, student loans, credit cards, and car loans divided by your pre-tax income. The higher your debt to income ratio the higher your mortgage interest rate will be. FHA's maximum qualifying debt ratios for borrowers in 2018 were 31% and 43% respectively. Which means the monthly housing payments on your mortgage should not exceed 31% of gross monthly income, while your total debt burden should not exceed 43% of your monthly pre-tax income. If you decide on purchasing your first home consider buying points to lower your interest rate on your home loan before closing on your first home. This can save hundreds of thousands of dollars in the long run and also decrease your financial burden in the long run. An interest rate of 3.25% or lower on a home loan can be achieved in any economy for a price if you buy interest points before you close on your first home. This may end up saving you thousands of dollars in the future.

THE FASTEST WAY TO COVER YOUR DEBT

Locum Tenens

The concept of locum tenens or temporary healthcare assignments has been around since 1979 as a way to send physicians to rural and underserved locations. This option is great if you like flexibility, no politics, the freedom to choose, and the open road.

Locum tenens allows you to control your own schedule, find work between full-time jobs, and navigate personal life transitions. Because assignments can be as short as a few days or even a few shifts, physicians, nurse practitioners, and physician assistants will often work locum tenens in addition to a full-time job to earn extra money on the side. Some locum tenens assignments require travel while others may be available close to home. Locums appointments are available all across the USA and locums' assignments can be turned into working vacations. The best way to use Locums is to pay off your student loans and keep your clinical skills sharp.

The reason Locums assignments are the best way to pay off debt is because you get paid in Pre-tax dollars. The highest paid Locums assignments are often Nocturnists, night shift physicians, because these shifts are challenging to fill. Generally, rural facilities or those having trouble attracting candidates will pay more than facilities in ideal urban locations. The rule of supply and demand also works in medicine. If the supply is high, the pay is low and vice versa. Locums assignments pay for your travels by providing a rental car or paying for gas miles. They will also pay for a hotel stay if you have to drive more than two hours for your shift.

Working as an Independent contractor also prevents you from losing your skills. If you work in a primary care office setting for at least two years, you will start losing your inpatient knowledge and skills, but by signing up with a Locums Tenens agency, you can keep your skills current by doing a few in-patient shifts a year.

Positions that include difficult procedures or require specialized skills often pay more than general assignments. Patient load also plays a role in pay — slower-paced assignments tend to pay less than high workload positions unless the slower pace assignments are located in high demand low supply areas. Though rates can vary, locum tenens providers generally earn a higher hourly rate than their full-time employees. According to recent data, average salary across all specialties, physicians who work locum tenens make more per hour than permanent-only doctors. Some of the highest paid states (from highest to lowest) are Indiana, Oklahoma, Connecticut, Wisconsin, Nevada, Arkansas, Louisiana, Alabama, Kentucky, and Florida.

Contracts that are called 1099 contracts pay employees in pre-tax dollars. You will work independently providing your services to a specific organization while you are compensated at a higher per hourly rate with no taxes taken out. As an Independent Contractor, you provide services to hospitals, nursing homes, and urgent care clinics.

Tax Implications

You may work through a Locums Agency or through your own independent limited liability company (LLC). In the United States, any company or organization engaged in a trade or business that pays more than $600 to an independent contractor in a year is required to report this to the IRS as well as the contractor using form 1099. This form states money paid to an independent contractor. Independent contractors do not have income taxes withheld like regular employees. Before you decide to form an LLC or work for a Locums Tenens Agency, consult with a tax professional to make sure you won't end up with a high tax liability at the end of the year.

The Drawbacks of Locums Tenens

Locum tenens can be quite lucrative, but there is one drawback you must consider.

Your salary is all you receive, there are no additional benefits. There is no IRA, 401K, medical, dental or eye insurance. You will need to purchase these benefits independently.

However, even with that one drawback, Locums Tenens is still a great way to clear up student loan debts. I think this is the best and fastest way. Unfortunately, I did not use this method because I discovered this after all my debts were paid via my W2 income. If you include this strategy in your debt repayment plan, you could pay off your debt faster than I did.

Think about it, you pay taxes once a year after you generate your revenue from the year prior. The tax you pay in 2019 is based on your income in 2018. For example, if you have pre-tax dollars or locums tenens income and you gross $300,000 for the year, you can put two-thirds ($200,000) on your student loans, or if you are a risk taker put all of it and work the spring of 2019 to pay for your taxes owed. Therefore, you can pay more towards your debt faster than your W2 after-tax income. However, be careful because this requires serious discipline and organization.

Since you do not obtain benefits such as health insurance you can try getting this benefit through your spouse's employer or purchase this on your own. If you would like to lower your taxes even further, I would suggest creating a limited liability company for your independent contractor business to have more income towards your debt.

If you choose to pay off your debt via your W2 income, you will have less money to go towards your debt. For example, your gross of $300,000 for the year with taxes taken out each month (roughly 40% of your income) will leave you with $180,000 for the year toward your debt.

However, let's be honest. The majority of physicians' salary for internist and family medicine doctors start at around $180,000 - $200,000. So, if you are left with 60% of your income after taxes each month, this will leave you with less money to cover your debt. If you are an independent contractor and have an LLC, you will lower your tax burden and have more money towards your debt. Even if you don't create an LLC and choose to work with a locum tenens agency instead, you have one year of pre-tax income to go towards your student loans, and you can use the following year months' work to pay your taxes owed to the IRS. For example, if you make $21,000 per month before taxes, this is money you can place entirely on your debt and save next month to cover taxes. If you use after-tax income, you will have $12,600 towards your debt. So, using pre-tax dollars is a faster way to lower your debt and lower the interest accruing on your principal. Once your debt is cut in half or eliminated, you can set aside a few months to work for Uncle Sam and cover your taxes. You can pay your taxes for your 1099 work via automatic data processing, ADP can manage your payroll even if you are the only employee in your company. You can have taxes calculated, deducted and paid automatically even with quarterly and annual reporting.

GOLDEN HANDCUFFS

So, you have spent your entire youth trying, becoming, and practicing being a fully trained professional. You made it to the finish line, now what? Just before you sign a contract for your first "real job" here comes the roadblock. However, before I get into the big stuff. Let's talk about time off. Of course, you're not used to time off, but hey it would be nice since you spent your entire youth studying. With that in mind, there are three types of agreements you can sign between you and your employer—No freedom, more freedom and that is enough freedom already.

No Freedom

A company may want you for themselves and them alone. All of your knowledge and talents for them for the rest of your life, if possible. This is often masked as intellectual property, anything related to medicine that you discover or come up with while working for a particular company belongs to them.

Some employment contracts require all your privacy disclosed to your new employer. Any agreement made with any other organization in the field of medicine must be shared, and if you fail to do so they will sue you, and you may have to cover the legal fees. This means no financial interest or practicing medicine outside of your employer can exist. By the time the ink dries on your agreement all your medical endeavors outside of your employer can no longer continue. Any income generated from the practice of medicine outside of your employer is illegal. Hint: these companies usually pay very well as you trade money for your freedom. Beware of the restrictive covenants and a big sign on bonus. I would suggest having a lawyer review and fully explain your contract before signing. I would recommend these companies only if you are older or can't see yourself doing anything else other than practicing medicine.

The upside is that these companies may let you leave the agreement without restriction upon the time of termination or resignation. These companies also tend to have excellent benefits packages and generous salary as a tradeoff for your intellectual property.

A Little More Freedom

You may not be able to work for any other medical practice or provide services to patients or be an entrepreneur without consent from your employer at your employer's discretion during your employment. Scary isn't it, but this too is negotiable. Even if you leave your employer, your employer may still own you for a few years based on restrictive covenants and non-compete clauses embedded in your contract. Make sure you read the fine print. You may not be allowed to provide any services, own your own business or be employed or invest in any company, which you came in contact with while working for your employer. Non-solicitation agreements may still exist even after you leave your employer. You will also not be able to work with any company that your ex-employer competes with, which is where the non-compete clause comes in. Often time's employers do not list their competitor, and you may not be able to work with their competitors even after you leave the company. Hint: these companies may pay a little more than your least restrictive companies, but you are usually bounded by the state that you are contracted in. If you want to leave you may have to move to a different state.

Others may allow you to practice with other companies or on your own whichever you choose. This means moonlighting or providing medical services when not scheduled to work. Restrictive covenants may still exist after the termination of your agreement. Some employers may give you months or even years in which you are not able to work within a certain distance of your previous employer, practicing the role you signed up for with your old employer. These employers usually pay the least, but you have more freedom to do whatever you choose outside of your employer.

Physician Staffing Companies

The benefits of working with physician staffing companies is that they often cover a multitude of hospitals within a particular geographic region. With that benefit, you can obtain credentialing at a variety of hospitals as an independent contractor while you navigate through the same company. You will also be able to pick up shifts at multiple healthcare facilities and obtain your income from one company versus numerous groups. If you become a full-time employee with one of these companies, you will be limited to the same pay and benefits as long as you are credentialed in a hospital they are affiliated with. If the same company has independent contractors working in the same hospital you will not be able to work as an independent contractor.

The drawback of being a full-time employee with a hospitalist staffing companies is that the hospitalist staffing companies are not considered a part of the hospital and undergo contract negotiations every few years. Physician staffing companies also entail ICU staffing and emergency medicine. Physician staffing companies area lucrative business and companies often compete against each other to obtain hospital contracts. As hospitals try to achieve the highest quality labor at the lowest possible cost, the staffing company may change every few years. Because of this, the company you are contracted with may lose their contract, and like a domino effect, you will lose your job or be offered a new contract with the winning company. With that said, it is best to discuss non-solicitation agreements with your staffing company in the event this occurs. If there is a non-solicitation agreement, you may not be able to secure a job with the hospital once the staffing company loses their contract. A non-solicitation agreement is a contract in which you agree not to try and obtain or be part of a hospital for your benefit or the benefit of a competitor after leaving your contracted company.

Often the hospital may decide to hire their own highly skilled labor, aka physicians. If you were already contracted with the hospitalist group and the hospital has not renewed the contract with the group, the hospital will have to "purchase" you from the hospitalist group at a hefty price tag.

Before signing contracts also consider non-compete agreements which are merely a contract between you and your employer. The contract prevents you from working for your current or future employer's competitor and from divulging information and processes of the contracting employer. A non-compete agreement protect a company's legitimate business interests and property. Without such agreement, companies fear that you may leave and compete with them.

Create Your Debt Elimination Plan

Use the worksheets in this section to track your journey to debt freedom.

Determine YOUR DISCRETIONARY INCOME

How much money you will have to put towards your debt repayment will depend on how much discretionary income you have. Your discretionary income is the amount of money you have left over each month after you have paid your living expenses. Use the chart below to list your monthly income and monthly living expenses (rent/ mortgage, utilities, car payments, insurance, food, clothing, etc.)

How much discretionary income do you have?

INCOME	
	$
	$
	V
	$
	$
	V
	$
	$
TOTAL INCOME	$

LIVING EXPENSES	
	$
	$
	$
	$
	$
	$
	$
	$
TOTAL EXPENSES	$

How much discretionary income do you have?

Total Income	-	Total Expenses	=	Discretionary Income

TIP: if your discretionary income is not as much as you'd like it to be, consider lowering your living expenses by remembering the Golden Rule!

Debt Record

Debt: ______________ Loan: $ ______________ Loan Period: ______________

Interest Rate: ____________________ % Fixed/Variable ____________________

No. of Repayments P.A.: ____

Minimum Monthly/Fortnight/Weekly Repayment: $ ________________________

Total Interest Payable: $ ____

Actual Repayment Amount: $ ____

REPAYMENT	DUE	PAID	BALANCE	REPAYMENT	DUE	PAID	BALANCE

Debt: ______________ Loan: $ ______________ Loan Period: ______________

Interest Rate: ____________________ % Fixed/Variable ____________________

No. of Repayments P.A.: ____

Minimum Monthly/Fortnight/Weekly Repayment: $ ________________________

Total Interest Payable: $ ____

Actual Repayment Amount: $ ____

REPAYMENT	DUE	PAID	BALANCE	REPAYMENT	DUE	PAID	BALANCE

Debt: ______________ Loan: $ ______________ Loan Period: ______________

Interest Rate: ____________________ % Fixed/Variable ____________________

No. of Repayments P.A.: ____

Minimium Monthly/Fortnight/Weekly Repayment: $ ________________________

Total Interest Payable: $ ____

Actual Repayment Amount: $ ____

REPAYMENT	DUE	PAID	BALANCE	REPAYMENT	DUE	PAID	BALANCE

Debt: ______________ Loan: $ ______________ Loan Period: ______________

Interest Rate: ____________________ % Fixed/Variable ____________________

No. of Repayments P.A.: ____

Minimium Monthly/Fortnight/Weekly Repayment: $ ________________________

Total Interest Payable: $ ____

Actual Repayment Amount: $ ____

REPAYMENT	DUE	PAID	BALANCE	REPAYMENT	DUE	PAID	BALANCE

Debt: ______________ Loan: $ ______________ Loan Period: ______________

Interest Rate: ____________________ % Fixed/Variable ____________________

No. of Repayments P.A.: ____

Minimum Monthly/Fortnight/Weekly Repayment: $ _______________________

Total Interest Payable: $ ____

Actual Repayment Amount: $ ____

REPAYMENT	DUE	PAID	BALANCE	REPAYMENT	DUE	PAID	BALANCE

Debt: ______________ Loan: $ ______________ Loan Period: ______________

Interest Rate: ____________________ % Fixed/Variable ____________________

No. of Repayments P.A.: ____

Minimum Monthly/Fortnight/Weekly Repayment: $ _______________________

Total Interest Payable: $ ____

Actual Repayment Amount: $ ____

REPAYMENT	DUE	PAID	BALANCE	REPAYMENT	DUE	PAID	BALANCE

Debt: ______________ Loan: $ ______________ Loan Period: ______________

Interest Rate: ____________________ % Fixed/Variable ____________________

No. of Repayments P.A.: ____

Minimium Monthly/Fortnight/Weekly Repayment: $ ________________________

Total Interest Payable: $ ____

Actual Repayment Amount: $ ____

REPAYMENT	DUE	PAID	BALANCE	REPAYMENT	DUE	PAID	BALANCE

Debt: ______________ Loan: $ ______________ Loan Period: ______________

Interest Rate: ____________________ % Fixed/Variable ____________________

No. of Repayments P.A.: ____

Minimium Monthly/Fortnight/Weekly Repayment: $ ________________________

Total Interest Payable: $ ____

Actual Repayment Amount: $ ____

REPAYMENT	DUE	PAID	BALANCE	REPAYMENT	DUE	PAID	BALANCE

Debt Snowball Worksheet

1. List your debts in order from lowest balance to largest balance.
2. Each month, you will pay the minimum balance on all of your debts and put any additional discretionary income you have towards your debt with the lowest balance.
3. As you pay off each debt, you snowball the payments you made into the next highest debt, while maintaining the minimum balances on the remaining debts.
4. Continue this practice until all of your debts have been paid off.

DEBT NAME	TOTAL AMOUNT OWED	MINIMUM PAYMENT DUE	DEBT SNOWBALL PAYMENT	NEW BALANCE					
				MONTH 1	MONTH 2	MONTH 3	MONTH 4	MONTH 5	MONTH 6

Keep it up…

Don't give up until you reach the finish line!

DEBT NAME	TOTAL AMOUNT OWED	MINIMUM PAYMENT DUE	DEBT SNOWBALL PAYMENT	NEW BALANCE					
				MONTH 7	MONTH 8	MONTH 9	MONTH 10	MONTH 11	MONTH 12

Debt Repayment Thermometer

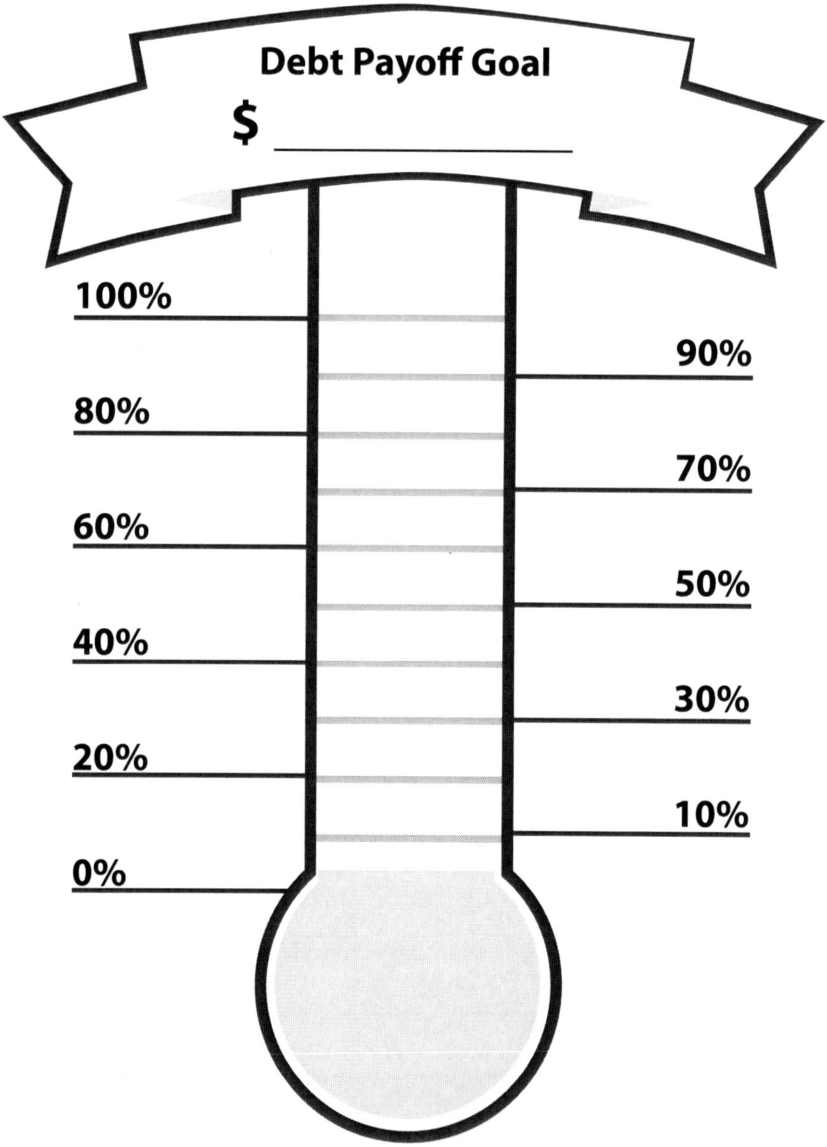

SURVIVING YOUR FIRST YEAR

I wish I would have known half of the things I will share with you in this section before I started my first year after residency. Not only does medical school not teach you about getting out of debt and obtaining financial freedom, it also doesn't prepare you to successfully navigate all of the intricacies of practicing medicine that go beyond treating patients.

In this section I'm sharing with you key tips and strategies that will help you to not only survive your first year, but thrive as well.

THE HOSPITALISTS

Who is a hospitalist?

A hospitalist is an internal medicine physician who practices medicine in the hospital setting. Hospital medicine is a type of practice within internal medicine in which the focus is on caring for hospitalized patients. Although not all hospitalists are required to be internists, the nature of internal medicine training uniquely prepares internists for hospital medicine practice. As a result, the vast majority of hospitalists are trained in internal medicine, usually general internal medicine.

The discipline of hospital medicine grew out of the increasing complexity of patients requiring hospital care and the need for dedicated clinicians to oversee their management. By focusing on this specific group of patients, hospitalists gain specialized knowledge in managing very ill patients and provides quality, evidence-based, and efficient patient and family-centered care in hospital settings.

A standard model involves working from one to two-week blocks of time followed by an equal amount of time off, which allows continuity of patient care throughout the majority of hospital admissions as well as enough time to decompress from the intensity of providing in-patient care. The most common practice is seven days on and seven days off.

Hospitalists may also focus their practice further within hospital medicine. Hospitalists who work primarily overnight are called Nocturnists. Hospitalists are employed by medical institutions to provide in-patient services, while others may be part of larger group practices to admit patients from within the practice who require hospital care. An important aspect of hospital medicine is the ability to collaborate and communicate with other physicians providing longitudinal care to ensure continuity between in-patient and ambulatory settings.

Teaching hospitals usually have medical students and internal medicine residents rotating on hospitalist-directed services, allowing the opportunity to teach. Some hospitalists, mostly in academic settings, perform research that may focus on treatment of specific diseases or investigation of care delivery models.

Hospitalists are also uniquely qualified to participate in or lead important hospital activities such as quality and patient safety initiatives. Most internists practicing hospital medicine are board certified in internal medicine. Although this is a most common level of training among practicing hospitalist internists, the American Board of Internal Medicine offers a specific certification called Focused Practice in Hospital Medicine for established internists who limit their practice to hospital medicine.

Hospitalists can be considered the backbone of the hospital working with other specialties to coordinate care of patients admitted to the hospital. These are some of the measures hospitalists are measured on while they care for patients.

Meeting attendance

Most companies would like you to be a part of a committee, and this requires you to attend meetings to come up with new ideas to improve healthcare on a weekly or monthly basis. Your meeting attendance may influence your role in becoming a partner within a hospitalist staffing company.

Sepsis Compliance

Sepsis occurs when a patient is admitted to the hospital with a fever (temperature greater than 38.3 degrees Celsius or 100.9 degrees Fahrenheit), hypothermia (core temperature less than 36.0 degrees Celsius), heart rate greater than 90 beats per minute, tachypnea, altered mental status, significant edema, hyperglycemia, leukocyte count greater than 12,000/uL, leukopenia (leukocyte count less than4000/uL), lactate greater than 1meq/L, platelet count less than 100,000/ul, and hypotensive.

Because sepsis is a significant issue in a hospital setting and a medicare quality measure hospitals need to stay on top of, time management and sepsis management protocols for reimbursements (getting paid for time management and correction of Sepsis).

HCAHPs

Hospitalists are also measured on HCAHPs (Hospital Consumer Assessment of Healthcare Providers and Systems) scores and your productivity bonus provided by your employer sometimes depends on it. The Centers for Medicare and Medicaid have developed 12 HCAHPs star ratings to make it easier for patients to use the information on the Hospital Compare website and to spotlight excellence in healthcare quality. Using data from 11 HCAHPS measure publicly reported on Hospital Compare, CMS created 11 HCAHPS star ratings. Topics include Doctor communication, Nurse communication, and responsiveness of hospital staff, pain management, communication about medicines, discharge information, care transition, cleanliness of hospital environment, the quietness of hospital environment, hospital ratings and willingness to recommend the hospital. So, what is the purpose of the HCAHPS Survey? It is a standardized survey instrument and data collection methodology that has been in use since 2006 to measure patient's perspectives of hospital care. It is a national standard for collecting and publicly reporting information that enables valid comparisons to be made across all hospital institution to support consumer choice. The HCAHPS sampling protocol is designed to capture consistent information on hospital care from the patient's perspective.

Re-admissions

October 2012, CMS began reducing Medicare payments for Inpatient Prospective Payment System (IPPS) hospitals with excess readmissions. A ratio measures excess readmissions, by dividing a hospital's number of "predicted" 30-day readmissions for heart attack, heart failure, pneumonia, COPD, Orthopaedic Surgery, and coronary artery bypass graft surgery by the number that would be expected, based on an average hospital with similar patients. A ratio higher than one indicates excess readmissions. Excess readmissions ratio is calculated by dividing the risk-adjusted predicted readmissions by the risk-adjusted expected readmissions. So, if a physician discharges a patient from the hospital and the patient returns to the hospital for a different or same chief complaint or diagnosis within 30 days, the hospital does not get paid or reimbursed.

PCP identification

Hospitalists are also graded on their ability to identify a patient's primary care physician once they enter the hospital. This is necessary because the primary care physician can know what medical condition the patient is currently being treated for and can prepare a plan for the patient once the patient is discharged from the hospital in an event to reduce hospital re-admission and to improve continuity of care on discharge. So, what do primary care physicians do? Primary care is often considered a traditional role for many Internal Medicine Physicians. Primary care involves first contact care for people with an undiagnosed symptom, sign, or health concern; care for individuals who are not problem- specific; longitudinal or continuous care; and responsibility for coordinating other health services related to a patient's care. Because internal medicine training is comprehensive and focused mostly on adults, general internists are particularly well equipped to provide preventive care, diagnose and treat disease in a primary care setting.

Primary care may be provided in a wide range of practice settings. Traditional primary care practices tend to be office-based, with internists either limiting their work to ambulatory settings or also managing their patients in the hospital when necessary. For those who define their work to the out-patient setting, arrangements are often made with hospitalists to help in caring for their patients requiring inpatient care. However, there are many other primary care practice types including combined subspecialty-primary care practices and combinations of primary care with different forms of practice. Many internists also have unique individualized primary care practice arrangements, including part-time and shared positions.

As with other types of internal medicine practice, general internists practicing primary care have the opportunity to participate in practice and quality improvement activities. Some primary care general internists participate in clinical research, and many also teach medical students and resident trainees in primary care settings.

Most internists practicing primary care hold the basic certification in internal medicine. They may also seek additional training to better address specific types of clinical issues or group of patients within their practice, such as geriatric medicine, sports medicine, or women's health.

ACP

Medicare Part B (Medical Insurance) covers voluntary advance care planning as part of the Yearly "Wellness" visit. This is planning for the care you'd want to get if you become unable to speak for yourself. An advance directive is just a written document stating how you want medical decisions to be made if you lose the ability to make them for yourself. It may include a living will and a durable power of attorney for health care. Which is important for patients who have multiple co-morbidities and frequent readmissions, especially geriatric patient greater than age 65. This discussion is needed early to prevent unnecessary intubation and resuscitation in the event a cardiac arrest or respiratory failure.

Anticipated discharge

Anticipated discharges are necessary to accelerate the discharge process. They assist the hospital social workers and case managers in preparing for safe and timely discharge, thereby decreasing patient's hospital length of stay and making sure they have all the tools at home to prevent unnecessary hospital readmission.

Discharge Orders before noon

Discharge orders before noon are essential so that all documents and communication can be completed so that the patient will most likely be discharged home. If discharge orders are put in late, these orders might be missed, and due to change of shift, discharges may be postponed until the next day, which will increase the length of stay.

TYPES OF PRACTICES

There are so many medical practice areas—how do you choose just one?

You have most likelyresearched a variety of private and group practice options. However, let's explore two that may new physicians don't consider.

Concierge Medicine

Concierge medicine is when a doctor or group of doctors charge a membership fee before they will see a patient or accept a patient into their practice. When a patient pays this fee, they get some services or amenities that Medicare doesn't cover, however they must still follow all Medicare rules.

Doctors who accept assignments can't charge you extra for Medicare-covered services. This means the membership fee can't include additional charges for items or services that Medicare usually covers unless Medicare won't pay for the item or services. Practices must provide their patients with an "Advance Beneficiary Notice of Non-coverage" (ABN) listing the services and reasons why Medicare may not pay. Practices who don't accept assignment can charge patients greater than the Medicare-approved amount for Medicare-covered services, but there's a 15% limit called the "Limiting Charge." All Medicare doctors can charge for items and services that Medicare doesn't cover. Patients pay 100% of their membership fee for concierge care. Most concierge practices are all cash only practices and do not accept insurance.

Urgent Care

An urgent care practice can be a great choice, especially if you are a family medicine physician because you have the freedom to see patients of all ages.

Urgent care facilities first opened in the United States during the 1970s. Emergency medicine physicians started many centers due to the public need for convenient access to medical care without being subjected to the extremely high costs traditional emergency rooms. Both the Urgent Care Association of America and the American Academy of Urgent Care Medicine have established criteria for urgent care centers. They must accept walk-in patients during business hours. They have to treat a broad spectrum of diseases and injuries, as well as perform minor medical procedures. Urgent care practices must have a licensed physician operating as the medical director and must be open seven days a week with on-site diagnostic equipment, including phlebotomy and X-ray, and contain multiple exam rooms.

Of the physicians that staff urgent care centers, almost 50% are family physicians, 30.1% are emergency medicine, and a small 7.6% are internal medicine.

The benefit of working as an urgent care physician is the flexibility to choose your hours and not having to worry about patient follow-ups after the acute care of your patients as in traditional office work. As an urgent care physician, you are expected to see two to four patients per hour for eight to twelve-hour shifts.

Drawbacks are that they tend to make less money than Hospitalists. However, you don't have to worry about the length of stay and discharges before noon. In recent years, the American Medical Association approved the UCM (Urgent Care Medicine) code. This code allows physicians to self-designate as specialization in urgent care medicine. Services rendered in an urgent care center may be designated using the place of service code on the CMS-1500 form, as submitted to third-party payers.

The Centers for Medicare and Medicaid Services have identified two specific codes that apply to urgent care centers: S9083 (global fee for urgent care centers) and S9088 (services rendered for Urgent care center).

With all the variables measured above for Physicians and Hospitals. A practicing physician in a hospital setting has to take care of at least 20 patients a day while considering all these variables. Office-based physicians also have to meet a goal of 20-30 patients a day. Office-based physicians may not have to deal with inpatient measures that Hospitalists are measured on, but they have a slew of checkboxes that must be covered to get reimbursed from Medicaid/Medicare and other insurance companies that have to be satisfied outside of patient care to be reimbursed for services provided.

THE REPLACEABLE IRREPLACEABLE

As hospitals scavenge to save money and companies try to remain profitable, physicians and nurses are caught in the middle.

Imagine signing your first contract with a hospitalist staffing company and thinking, "I'm going to work seven days on and have seven days off for rest."

Seems lovely, doesn't it?

However, on your fifth day of work, you are called at 9 pm the night before your next shift and told. "Doc, Good evening, the patient census at the hospital is low. We don't need you."

Remember, if you don't work, you don't get paid. You find yourself scavenging for open shifts to keep up with the monthly budget you have set for yourself.

Companies and hospitals need you—until they don't. This is what is done to their full-time employees. Physicians get dragged back and forth regarding necessities. Companies do this too in the outpatient settings. For example, in the outpatient setting, a contract salary is promised for the first two years of guaranteed pay and then after two years, your salary is based on the number of patients you are able to see minus the cost of overhead. This means that the number of patients you see determines your income and you are responsible based on your patient volume to cover the cost of your employer's overhead. Doesn't seem fair, does it? But, it's business.

Capitalists also have a golden rule—those who have the gold make the rules.

Most people know there is a play going on out in the world, but they don't understand it. This is frequently the experience of Locums Physicians. Because you are an independent contractor, your work is not guaranteed and can be canceled at any time. It would be great if you can negotiate your cancellation policy with your contracted company. A few days' notice would be nice so you can make other arrangements.

A way to avoid being pulled back and forth is to work the night shift as a Nocturnist in a hospital setting or work in a nursing home setting. These jobs are usually not desired because the idea of not getting sleep at night and working with the elderly who have multiple co-morbidities does not seem practical to most. However, the benefit is that if you are not available, no one else is readily available to do your job. The patients in a nursing home are fixed so there is always work for you to do. As a Nocturnist in a hospital, the hospital is usually understaffed at night, and no one else can do your job, so you are unlikely to get canceled.

SHOW ME THE MONEY

Productivity pays.

The more patients you see in a given day, the more money you can make. Companies use Relative Value Units (RVUs) and productivity bonuses to reward physicians who can attend to more patients. Theroectically, this sounds like a great way to make extra money, however companies don't make it easy for you to meet their standards for the bonuses and you must be extremely diligent in monitoring yrou paychecks to make sure your pay is accurately calculated.

Typically, in a hospital setting, physicians are expected to see fifteen patients per day. If your hospital census per provider is twenty patients, your productivity and RVU will increase your salary. However, you may frequently have to examine each pay stub you receive as accountants often make mistakes when they are calculating your pay as they have more variables to work with.

Some companies may make you wait three months before receiving your RVU and bonus. This makes it hard for you to check errors on income earned and you may be paid less than your contract agreement in some instances. They may also make you jump through a lot of administrative hoops before you can receive your RVU and productivity bonus, such as charting compliance and meeting attendance. I f you miss one thing, they will have a reason not to give you your RVU and productivity bonuses.

RVUs and productivity bonuses are variables that you may or may not receive based on what the company feels is in their best interest. They may also offer you a high per shift pay rate after completing a certain number of shifts while maintaining their quality standards.

What if I don't want ot deal with the hassle of RBUs and productivity bonuses?

There are companies that will give you a standardized salary with no RVU or productivity bonuses. The upside to this is that what you see is what you get, nothing more, nothing less. Other companies will try to pay you a large or comfortable salary, but you will be under a wide range of restrictive covenants and patients that you are managing will often have 24 hours access to you until they are no longer under your care. Meaning, if you are home after completing your 12-hour shift at a hospital and something happens in the hospital setting, look forward to a call until you have discharged your patient.

The upside to this is that if patients have 24-hour access to you, your census load is usually less, 5-8 patients for a hospital setting.

THE NURSING HOME HOSPITALIST

Nursing homes have started to mimic the hospital model, calling it "Sub-acute Hospitalist." In this model, you will have 20 patients in the nursing home setting that you have to round on daily. RVUs and productivity bonuses are earned after you see more than 20 patients for the day which is often not possible.

THE NOCTURNIST

A noc-what?

Many people still don't know what a nocturnist is. A nocturnist is simply an internal medicine physician who works the night shift in a hospital setting versus the regular day shift. A shift usually consists of 12 hours from 7 pm to 7 am.

I was led to my career as a nocturnist by the urge to practice pure medicine without feeling as if I am working for the insurance companies in an office setting or working as an expert discharger in the day setting.

The first week as a nocturnist is the hardest part. I experienced a lot of adrenaline at night, but when I went home, I crashed and had difficulty waking up in the evenings. I had to pull myself from bed and drag myself to get ready for work. Admitting 8-10 patients at night while covering half the hospitalized patient in a 350 plus bed hospital while at the same time responding to codes was not an easy task. I also had to update the census in the morning before the day hospitalists arrived to start their 12 hours shifts. I almost felt like quitting, but after the first week, I finally got the hang of it.

What I also realized working as a Nocturnist is that the staff at your hospital can try and destroy you. Your employer may not care that you are the best doctor, you are saving lives, preventing lawsuits by tackling and controlling situations. I was covering a 350 plus bed hospital with shared responsibility with another nocturnist while being responsible for nine admissions each at night, reporting to rapid responses and code blues and requests from the floor for symptomatic management of patients at night. Then I get a text from the Chief. "Doctor, you were written up by the ER Doc and the nurse because you took too long to call back."

What?

Think about it - two nocturnists with more than 100 patients each, Rapid response, emergency coverage and admissions, two pagers attached to our hips throughout the night.

One pager is for floor management, the other to cover half the hospital while another nocturnist has a pager to cover the other half of the facility and to respond to codes. We rotate the emergency response pager and the admission pager every 3 hours until our 12-hour shift is completed.

So, I admit I was upset because they know that it is skeleton labor at night. No one cares that you are in the middle of an emergency. No one wants to wait for 5 minutes for a call back from the hospitalist.

You are also responsible for consults from other specialties at night. For example: Surgery and Ob/GYN. However, the rule at night is everyone wants the hospitalist STAT. Now. Fast.

How can one nocturnist who has so much responsibility please everyone?

I finally figured it out. I decided that at the beginning of the shift I am going to call each floor, each section I cover and ask does anyone need the nocturnist covering. Then, I would do these floor calls every 3 hours during the night and a half an hour before my shift ends. So, whether paged or not, they will get a call from me checking in.

I recommend calling the Emergency Room when it's your time to do admissions even before the ER pages you andask if you are needed. You have a quota for admissions you are expected to do at night, so you might as well get to it. If you wait for them to call you, you might be with a patient or responding to a code.

The truth is, no one cares, and if they can't get you they get upset and then start complaining, and before you know it, they have written you up to the Big Boss even if you call back in 2 minutes.

Hospitals have systems set up for instant reporting by nurses, clerks, and other physicians in which they can file a complaint immediately to your superior, Chief Medical Officer and CEO. These complaints stay on your file. You can even be written up by staff members due to your tone of voice used on the floors and during interaction with staff and colleagues.

Half an hour before your shift ends, I recommend calling each floor and say "Does anyone need the nocturnist?"

If the answer is no, there is no way they could ever say they paged and couldn't get you or you took too long to respond. This way you control the pages instead of the pages controlling you.

You take back control and end up having an excellent reputation for checking in, and everyone is less frustrated. You get an excellent reputation for non- medical management, which seems to matter more by the staff than medical management.

We live in a people pleasing, demanding, me too society where everyone likes to point fingers and blame, so flip the script. Reach out before they decide to reach out to you, then they could never say you were not available. Timed calls are like timed voids in geriatrics, it prevents a fall and makes you keep your credentials and image at a hospital.

So, it's almost coming to the end of my first year working as nocturnist in a hospital setting, and I have to say I enjoy taking care of hospitalized patients at night. I feel like it's the heart of medicine. I was treating real people, not the insurance companies.

If you can overlook your circadian rhythm being thrown for a loop and getting over 100 pages from the floors for silly things like cough medicine and sleeping pills, you'll be just fine. However, in some strange reality, I feel like this is one of the few ways you can escape the increasing demands of the insurance companies, the ten variables you are continuously being measured on example, length of stay, discharges before noon and the list goes on and on. As a nocturnist, you are responsible for admitting patients once deemed necessary by the Emergency Room doctor, transferring patients from other outside hospitals for more acute care in the hospital settings, covering the floors at night and yes even do codes and respond to rapid responses.

TIPS FOR SURVIVING THE NIGHT SHIFT

1. **Invest in a quality portable dictating system.** Talking is faster than writing, even if you write 60 words per minute. You will be able to see your notes generated on the screen as you talk and be able to submit your history and physical examination notes right away. If you use a phone dictation system, this is often faster, but the only thing is that you may not be able to see your notes until the next day when it is uploaded into your EMR system.

2. **Familiarize yourself with as many EMR (Electronic Medical Record) and EHR (Electronic Health Record) codes as possible.** This will help you maneuver easily when you work and obtain credential and licensing at different health systems.

3. **Take a nap!** Trust me— I didn't do this, and it led to severe burnout. Even if it's only for 15-30 minutes, sit in a quiet, dark room and relax. This will increase your longevity in working the night shift.

4. **Negotiate your patient admissions.** The night shift is one of the only shifts where you can practice pure medicine without politics unless you fall short of your admissions quota.

5. **Write a progress note, code, and bill all your rapid responses, Internal Medicine Consults, and code blues for critical care time on the floor.** Meaning if it's critical, and you took time to assess, manage, and treat the patient, you can bill for it. This is important because if you bill for it, this gets counted as if you did an admission. Responding to emergencies on the floor may delay your ability to complete admissions from the emergency room, this way, all your work will be accounted for.

6. **Always give yourself credit and thank God you made it through the night.** It's not an easy job, but you get to practice everything you learned in medical school without someone watching you under a microscope because they are all sleeping, Thank God for that.

7. **Negotiate meeting attendance.** Asking a nocturnist to come to a meeting at 2 pm is like asking a hospitalist to come to a meeting at 2 am. Nobody wants to do that so why should you. They may make not showing up to meetings hold you back from getting your RVU's and Productivity Bonus. Trust me. It happened to me.

8. **Say Good Evening and Good Morning to everyone, especially the key players in the hospital.** Be nice to your nurses, nursing administrator, the receptionist who delegates calls on the floors between the hospi-

talists and the nurses. Be nice to your executive assistant and secretary. Remember, if you can't say it in front of your boss, don't say it behind your boss' back.

9. **The number of admissions you do during your shift will determine if your boss will replace you or the other nocturnist with a physician assistant.** Hospitals and businesses are the sharks in the shark tank. If you don't do admissions, they can't make any money, and if they can't make money, they may have to hire cheaper labor. These PAs and NPs will still need your Doctor License to work under so if this is the case and you are working with a PA or NP at night you may want to negotiate your contract again, after all, it is your license we are talking about. You want to keep your license clean and protected from default or someone else's negligence so you must protect it and learn how to negotiate.

10. **Start typing up a rough draft of your notes and save it even before you see your patients.** You can get a sense of what your case workup will be based on the information given to you by the ER physicians, the lab and imaging team, and the medication list shown on the patient profile. Templates are your best friend when it comes to doing admissions and charting. If you can create a template which has the basic set up for your CC (Chief Complaint), HPI (History of Present-

ing Illness), ROS (Review of Systems), PE (Physical Examination), A/P (Assessment and Plan) and have it automated into your progress notes, it will save you time when it comes to charting. More time is spent charting than with patients, so if you can narrow your charting time to a few minutes by creating templates, you will have more time for your patients and their families, and of course, there will be more rest time for you. Make friends with the Information Technology department at your hospital and have them teach you how to make templates.

11. **It would help if you had all billing and coding done at least 30 minutes before the hospitalist comes to work.** Your notes must be completed because their day begins the minute you leave and distribute the patients to each hospitalist in the morning.

12. **If the ER physicians call with new admissions for you, go to the Emergency Room and take the admissions (patients).** See all of the patients in the Emergency Room. They are right there in their little sections in the ER, and you won't have to spend time later going to each of their private rooms. Thus the majority of your work is almost halfway completed at the beginning of the night.

13. **Make sure you have a penlight to check pupillary reflexes when you pronounce a patient dead at**

night. If your hospital has chaplain services, use it. Ask the family if they would like a Chaplain to pray over their deceased loved ones. This will help them cope, and you can go back to seeing your assigned patients.

14. **Wear comfortable clothing—scrubs and sneakers.** You need to be efficient and fast on your feet at night. Some nocturnists wear suits that are as comfortable for them as wearing scrubs. If this is your personality, then, enjoy it as long as you are comfortable.

15. **Never work more than three nights in a row.** Twelve shifts a month should be considered full-time to prevent burnout. Night nurses work three shifts a week for many years. Nocturnist working seven nights on and seven nights off will lead to burnout and fatigue, especially if you pick up shifts in between.

16. **Monday nights are usually the busiest nights.**

17. **If your personality starts to change or you become more irritable in the months after starting your night shift, you may need a break.** Consider picking up some day shifts. Side effects of working nights are depression, panic attacks, burnout, and personality changes. It's recommended that you take a least one month vacation a year to reset. If you work three nights in a row, you will need three to four nights of

rest to reset your circadian rhythm.

18. **When you come home from your night shift—pray, eat, shower, and go to sleep right away.** Don't stay up looking at emails, watching television, online shopping if you have to wake up and go to work the following night. This will lead to chronic fatigue over time. Wear eye masks in the morning, so your eyes are not exposed to light when you are trying to initiate sleep. It is recommended for you to get eleven hours of rest after your night shift, even if that seems excessive to you.

19. **Keep the Sabbath holy, even if you are not a Christian.** Take a day of rest. This will help to prevent burnout.

MEET THE AUTHOR
KAMALA GORDON, MD, MBA

I started my life with big dreams, but not a lot of money. I saw how my parents, especially my mother, worked long hard hours to give my siblings and me a better life. Although my mom had big dreams of her own, her brutal work schedule kept her from pursuing them. She worked si much that she was never present physically for most of my childhood. I decided that when I grew up, I didn't want to live from pay check to pay check and that I wanted to have the freedom to pursue my dreams.

I grew up in Jamaica and went to Bradford Prep School. After graduating with honors, I received a scholarship for Titchfield High School where I majored in the sciences. I later went on as an International Student to Temple University where I majored in Biology and minored in Business and continued my journey to Medical School at AUA. I completed my Internal Medicine residency in Brooklyn, New York at Wyckoff Heights Medical Center (New York Medical College Program), and then continued on to complete my Fellowship in Geriatric Medicine at Temple University Hospital. I also obtained my MBA at Plymouth State University along the way.

I created this book to make your journey a little easier, so you can make informative decisions to propel your future in the direction you would like it to go.

I currently reside in the North East Coast with my husband and my pup.

LET'S STAY CONNECTED

Follow me on IG @thegalmd

For more resources, visit thegalmd.com

Made in United States
North Haven, CT
05 November 2026

21791731R00051